BREAD BAKING BIBLE

For Bread Bakers Apprentice

Maru Castilla

Copyright © 2014 Maru Castilla

All rights reserved.

ISBN-10: **1505258197**
ISBN-13: 978-1505258196

Table of Content

Basic Techniques

Base Mix "sponge" starter..3
    Tip: Heat..4
Treatment of the yeast...5
    Tip: The mixing..6
The art of mixing..7
    Tip: The Table..8
Shaping...9
Decorating the bread..10

Bread Recipes

WHITE BREAD

    Country Loaf..15
    Pizza Bread...16
    Carrot and herb bread..17
    Aniseed Braid..18
    Italian Bread..19

Tip: Cooking..20

The Chipaco..21

Oriental Steamed Bread..22

WHOLEMEAL BREAD

Wholemeal bread with sourdough........................27

    Tip: Options..28

Basic Organic Wholemeal Bread........................29

    Tip: Buns of Reference..................................30

Strasbourg Rye bread..31

Pumpkin Bread..32

Beer Bread..33

Swedish Bread..34

Tynbrod..35

Rye Baguettes..36

SWEET BREADS

Twisted filling..41

Wholewheat Croissants..43

Oat and chocolate Crunchies..45

Granola Nougat...46

Apple Cupcakes..47

Baked Cakes..48

STUFFED BREADS

Humita stuffed Bread...51

Bread stuffed with Chorizo..52

Ham Torzadas...53

Stuffed Croissants...54

FESTIVE BREADS

Pretzel...57

Corn bread...58

Oat and beer tortillas..59

Bagel..60

Special Focaccia...61

Rice Bread..62

BREAD BAKING BIBLE

Approximately 6,000 - 8.000 years ago bread was first kneaded, moistening the flour on stone. It is one of the oldest foods known of and endures to this day. Later, the Egyptians discovered yeast and then the Arabs the oven. Numerously mentioned in the Bible, bread is used symbolically in various religions. During the Middle Ages bakers were part of one of the most respected guilds, Parisians protesting rising bread prices started the French Revolution ... Currently one third of the world population consumes bread, regardless of social status or cultural level, as a staple.

Referring to the work ("You have to be a bread winner"), true love ("With you bread and onion") and newborns ("Arrived with bread under his arm") expresses the noble and good bread we want both for others and ourselves, as it not only provides substances that powers the body but has a soul that nourishes he who offers and who receives it.

Make your own bread, share it and receive and salute its benefits.

BASIC TECHNIQUES

Base Mix "Sponge" Starter

1 lt. of water   1 tbsp salt
6 tz. Flour   Neccesary flour
1 tbsp. Sugar or Honey   ½ cup oil
1 tbsp. yeast

In a bowl mix the room temperature water, flour and yeast, the water temperature should be at 35 degrees when you mix it in the container with the flour. The remaining ingredients are measured by heaped tablespoons. In the event that the yeast is dried, you should weigh 15 gr, while if it is compressed or fresh, it should be 50 grams that will be incorporated by crumbling it on the damp dough and mixing intensely .

The mixture should be left to rest for an hour, when it will have a spongy aspect.

Add the remaining ingredients following the order in which they are listed. As it thickens, wrap the dough from the edges toward the center before taking to the table to continue kneading it.Incorporate the oil as you stir and bring the oily mass to the previously floured table.

Kneed and strike it as detailed in The Kneading Technique.

At this stage the dough should be well covered with a polyethylene sheet and a fabric so as to prevent airflow between bread and plastic.

If the surface of the dough is elastic, it is because it is not yet ready to be baked, on the other hand, if it is deflated, it will have gone over. The point is ideal for baking when the dough feels soft to the touch.

HEAT
It is essential to keep the dough warm at the end of kneading. The dough only rises at room temperature or slightly warmer. It is likely that if you cut the dough into portions it will lower its temperature, so you should cover it quickly with nylon and cloth.

TREATMENT OF THE YEAST

The yeast is a unicellular microorganism, so that its working life is determined by a wet or liquid environment. At a temperature of between 20 and 35 degrees it ferments at an accelerated rate, quickly consuming stocks of oxygen and food. It is not good for this to happen during the first steps, but in the last leavening, because at 55 or 60 degrees the yeast dies and completes its cycle.

Leavened dough is a result of the yeast breathing as do our cells, absorbing oxygen from water on inhaling and exhaling carbon dioxide that is trapped in the interior of the dough. Sifting the flour or beating the mixture vigorously first can also provide air for the yeast.

Saccharomyces cereviciae is the name given to beer yeast, and means "sweet cereal fungus." This means that the yeast feeds on the sugars in the dough. Adding sugar or honey accelerates the process.

By providing oxygen and sugar to the dough you've developed the ideal performance environment for the dough and thus will achieve better bread. "rock hard"

THE MIXING

Serves to dilate and hydrate wheat proteins to bind them in an elastic mesh. When the flour is added all at once, the dough dries leaving the bread "rock hard".

THE ART OF MIXING

Facing the formless goo you should consider:
1. Our hands must be free of attached dough, to do this you must rub them with flour and incorporate those bits in to main mass.

2. You will knead it on the table we floured early, then the reduced amount of flour until the dough does not stick to the table. The idea is to create a progressive texture through stretching and spreading movements, adding flour solely on the table as the sudden addition of flour to the dough will dry it irreversibly.

3. If the pressure you exert on the dough during kneading is excessive, you will surely tear the dough and this is not good. Ideally, gently push following the rhythm of the dough when it stops yielding to our push.

4. Basic motions:

Folding: fold the dough in half bringing the far edge toward you.

Push: the heel of the palm pushes the mass forward, then unite the fold and roll the dough.

Rotate: rotate the dough 90 degrees to start again.

If the basic movements are done correctly the dough begins to take on a spherical shape , smooth and without folds.

5. When the dough starts to become elastic and does not adhere to the table, kneading can be alternated with a shock, that is, the mass is thrown from high up on to the table to relax the dough.

One routine can be push-turn-fold and give three blows so that the dough is stronger and softer.

THE TABLE

A strong wooden table is the perfect place for kneading.

If the surface where it is made is very cold, like marble or stone, one option is, before starting to knead, is to put a pot with hot water to warm up the surface.

Likewise, remember that water is what determines the temperature of the dough. In the case that the weather is cold, hot water should be added so that the resulting mixture is warm.

SHAPING

The time to do this is when the mass releases tension, ie when it rises and allows you to flatten it with the palm of the hand or with a rolling pin. The shaping should be carried out on a floured board.

If the result you want to obtain are flutes, roll the dough and press with palms.

Loaves are achieved by forming a bun and rolling it on the counter to make the dough spread. Complete along the length of the tin, without leaving empty spaces.

With a spatula or pastry cutter you can cut different shapes to prepare individual loaves.

Decorating the Bread

Before turning the dough out on to the counter, while it is sticky, you can tip it onto different seeds.

Once the bread is made it is easy to decorate it by placing two plates, one with seeds and another with water: slightly wet the bun in the first plate and continue by to resting the bread on the plate with the seeds, which will remain stuck on by the moisture.

Another option is to paint the loaves with a brush: thickening water with starch can attach various seeds, even larger than sesame seeds.

A practical way is to cut with scissors, knife or cutter on the surface. The cuts can draw pictures, be in the form of a cross, longitudinal, transverse or square.

An original decoration is to make little rolls and attach them to large loaves or also to the individual ones.

Flat breads are decorated by making holes, sinking the tips of your fingers into the dough and adorn with herbs and spices there.

BREAD RECIPE

CHAPTER

2

WHITE BREAD

COUNTRY LOAF

Ideally, cook it in a clay oven, after the pizzas and pies, when the heat is softer.

2 kg. flour 000   2 tbsp. of fine salt

400 grs. lard   2 tbsp. sugar

100 grs. fresh yeast   1 lt. of warm water

In a bowl mix the flour, salt and warm lard. Make a hole in the flour and add the crumbled yeast. Combine the sugar with the warm water and yeast folding it in while incorporating the flour slowly and stirring. Begin kneading while gradually incorporating the flour. Let the dough rest until it rises.

Take the dough and make an elongated shape and place it on the table or on a floured tray and Transfer it with a paddle to the clay oven.

Once it has risen, heat in the oven at medium heat for an hour and a half.

Pizza Bread

This bread is ideal as a starter while waiting for the main course. Sometimes people add cheese and ground pepper giving the pizza bread a slightly spicy flavor that complements well the intense flavour of the cheese

2 cups. flour 000	1 tsp. salt
1 cup. of warm water	4 tbsp. oil
1 tablespoon yeast	Fine salt
	Grated chees at your discretion

Place the dough on the counter, form a well in the center and add the yeast oil and salt there. Tip the water slowly so that it does not spill and add the ingredients with your fingertips. Knead intensely until the dough is smooth and tender.

Cover the dough with plastic wrap and let rise until it doubles in volume.

Stretch the dough until about 3 mm thick and place in an oiled pizza tray. Wet the surface with a tablespoon of warm salt water and sprinkle with grated cheese.

Mark 8 portions with a spatula. Leave a little to leaven and bake at very high heat until browned.

Accompany with beer while waiting for dinner.

CARROT AND HERB BREAD

500 gr. superfine white whole wheat flour

1 tbsp. salt

1 tbsp. yeast

1 tbsp. sugar

250 cc. milk

25 grs. butter

200 grs. grated carrots (thick)

2 tbsp. chopped parsley

Place in a bowl the flour, salt and sugar, mix and make a gap in the middle. Add warm milk and melted butter in the hollow formed. Beat along with the yeast, gradually adding the surrounding flour until it takes on a creamy consistency. Let it stand for a few minutes.

Continue stirring and adding flour until it becomes a smooth paste. Add the carrot with parsley and fold in with the flour. Shape and roll and lower it to the table.

Knead in the remaining flour until the dough becomes elastic. Note that carrot releases moisture, hence the kneading process is longer).Add more flour if you consider it necessary.Place dough in an oiled bowl and cover with plastic. Separating two or three portions to the dimensions of the molds. Let the dough rise until doubled in volume and bake in the oven bottom on a medium heat.

Share with family they are very nutritious

Aniseed Braid

Infallible at snack time, the presentation of this classicly shaped bread plait

500 grs. all-purpose flour	1 tbsp. yeast
½ tsp. Salt	1 ½ cup milk
20 grs. anise seeds (they can be crushed or powdered)	60 grs. butter
100 grs. sugar	1 egg
	1 egg yolk

Add anise to the milk, heat to boiling point and allow to cool.

Prepare a start with warm milk, some flour and yeast until you have a creamy texture. Let stand for 30 minutes covered with plastic.

Add the remaining ingredients at approximately 25 degrees (room temperature) and the remainder of flour gradually, until it separates from the edges of the bowl. Place on the table and knead for about 10 minutes. Divide into three portions and make round buns. Let rise for one hour covered with plastic.

After proofing, flatten with the palm of your hand each bun to degas them, stretch it until it forms a thick stick.

Take one of the long sides and begin to roll the dough tightly and make sticks about 70 cm long. Turn while stretching the dough so that it is cylindrical in shape and make a braid.

Italian Bread

A crumbly bread supersoft and open...

6 cups flour 000	20 trs. dry yeast
1 tbsp. salt	1/3 cup milk powder
1 tbsp. tablespoon malt extract	3 cup water
	1 tbsp. oil

Whisk yeast, malt and water. Add yeast, without stopping mixing and let stand a few minutes.

Incorporate into a bowl the flour with salt and form a well in the centre. Pour the previous mixture whisking vigorously with a wooden spoon until the dough is elastic and smooth.

Gradually incorporate the remaining flour until the mixture thickens and can be kneaded. Add the oil and scrape the bowl walls with a spatula.

Knead on a floured board and every so often sprinkle with flour.

When you notice that the dough becomes firmer and does not stick to the table, throw it hard on to the table. Continue alternating the kneading and blows for about 7 minutes more. Tip it in to the bowl and cover with plastic for 2 hours until risen.

With the tips of your fingers turn and degas the dough, cover again and let stand another hour.

Uncover, cut into two portions and knead each bun to desgas it for a few seconds. Give it a few blows to loosen and arrange on a floured tray with enough space for it to double in volume. With a sharp knife make decorative cuts and bake at high heat in the lower rack of the oven until golden.

COOKING
Salty doughs take colour more slowly than sweet doughs, so we must bake at medium heat for cooking to complete and not burn

The Chipaco

A traditional Country bread

1 ½ kg. all-purpose flour

½ cup. melted fat (or pork)

1 tbsp. salt

2 cups. greaves of the same fat

1 tbsp. yeast

Take the fat and cut it into cubes in a saucepan over a low heat until they are fried and have taken on a golden colour. Meanwhile, prepare a brine with a litre of warm water and a tablespoon of salt (fine). Once that the rinds are ready, separate them.

To the flour add yeast and mix, afterwards the fat and rinds. Gradually add the brine into a paste. Knead vigorously and then let the dough rest.

(This ideal bread to bake in a clay oven). Turn the oven on.

Cut the pastry into four portions and give them a round and flattened form: cover with a cloth and let it rise before baking.

ORIENTAL STEAMED BREAD

So easy and so fluffy

Ingredients

1 cup. Sourdoug

3 cup button. fine organic wholemeal flour

2 cup button. Hot water

1 ½ tsp ½. coarse sea salt

Materials

1 large saucepan with lid

1 separator from bottom of the pot(for steaming)

1 plate to separate the bread and separator

1 canvas 60cm x 60cm approx

1 wooden skewer

Place the flour in a terrine, open a hole in the center and add the remaining ingredients and the warm water, beat with a fork and add the flour gradually to form an elastic dough. Cover the dough and leave for about 20 minutes to become spongy.

Knead with what was left of the flour until it incorporates in to the dough, and if needed, use more flour to get a firm elastic bun.

Place it on a floured board, cover with plastic. Let it rest a while.

Remove the plastic and degas by flattening it with your palms. With a rolling pin stretch the dough to a thickness of 1 cm forming a square. Brush the surface with oil.

Roll it, remembering that the result should be a well compressed "sausage".

With a sharp knife, cut portions every 3 cm, forming small rolls.

Place one portion on top of another. Lay the wooden skewer (brochette type skewer) on the upper roll and press down firmly so that both rolls are joined.

Place the divider in the pot, pour in water and place a plate on the separator. Cover the bowl with a damp and folded cloth . There should be about 6-8 cm. clearance between the plate and the cover.

Preheat the pan a few minutes before cooking.

Arrange the rolls on the canvas and cook in the steaming covered pot for about 20 minutes.

WHOLEMEAL BREAD

WHOLEMEAL BREAD WITH SOURDOUGH

Ideally, you cook in clay oven after the pizzas and pies, when the heat is gentler.

2 kg. flour 000

400 grs. lard

100 grs. fresh yeast

2 tbsp. of fine salt

2 tbsp. sugar

1 lt. of warm water

Prepare a start with a base mix, 3 cups flour and water and let stand.Consider that the more you ferment bread (for a day) it will be more nutricious, have a much stronger flavor and keep for longer.Also, if you let it ferment for one hour, it results in a more open texture and a softer flavor.

When you decide to terminate the fermentation thicken the paste by adding honey, flour, sea salt and yeast. Cover the dough and leave in a warm place for an hour to ferment and it will give it an open texture.

To knead it more add flour and oil, working on the table until the dough does not stick and is elastic.Cover with plastic and leave for an hour to leaven.

Divide into portions and shape the type of bread you prefer. Place the bread on a tray, cover and let rise until they are ready.In a bowl mix the flour, salt and warm fat.Make a hole in the flour and add the crumbled yeast. Combine the sugar with the warm water and stir while tipping it on yeast. Begin kneading while gradually incorporating the flour. Let the dough rest until it rises slightly.

Take the dough and make a elongated bun. Put it on the table or on a floured tray and transfer it with a spatula to the clay oven.

Once it has risen, heat in the oven at medium heat for an hour and a half.

Serve before the meal accompanied a red wine and juicy anecdotes.

OPTIONS

The crispy crust counteracts the strong flavour, so if you feel that the dough is very acidic, it is preferable that the loaves are small, round or flattened.

Sunflower seeds nicely complement the taste: In a bowl with a base of well-salted water dip the bread and then roll them on another plate with seeds.

BASIC ORGANIC WHOLEMEAL BREAD

In this bread we use wheat flour grown without chemical additives, of natural selection. This is called wheat organic, that is, which is not transgenic

Starting ingredients

1 lt. water

4 cups medium organic wholemeal flour

2 cups. organic superfine flour

1 tbsp. honey or brown sugar

1 tbsp. yeast

To complete

1 tbsp. coarse sal

3 or 4 cups superfine wholemeal flour

½ cup. corn oil

1 cup of sesame seeds

In a bowl with water, put the flour gradually until the mixture thickens, add the yeast and honey; incorporate them stirring with a wooden spoon. Cover and let stand 30 to 60 minutes and you will have the start dough or sponge dough.

When it acquires a consistency of mousse throw in the remaining flour with the salt, then fold it in to the mix. Only when the dough is thick enough and falls away from the sides, add the oil and stir a bit more before taking to a floured board. Knead until it takes a firm consistency and throw it hard on to the table about three times. Alternate with kneading to tighten it and give it a stretchy texture.

When you notice it does not stick to the table, let it rest covered with plastic first and a cloth over it.

After an hour of rest, the dough will double in volume and you can now do rolls; again leave them covered for about 30 or 60 minutes.

Proceed to shape them and decorate them with the sesame seeds: dampening them and rolling the new buns on a plate covered with seeds. Hit on the table to accommodate the seeds and rid it of those which have not been well adhered. Again covered with plastic and fabric leave them to rise again.

Give them decorative cuts and place them in the oven for as long as the volume of the rolls requires

BUNS OF REFERENCE

Bread: 600 - 800 grams. (Depending on the size of the mold)

Rolls: 50 - 200 grams.

Pizzas: 300 - 500 grams.

Several Buns: de 500 grams. - 2 kg

Strasbourg Rye bread

Exquisitely fragrant bread because the fermentation aroma is accentuated with the passage of the days and the resulting bread is very tender

1 cup. rye flour (fine or coarse)

2 cups. thin rye flour

1 ½ cups warm water

20 grs. dry yeast

1 cup Hot water

1 tbsp. salt

1 tbsp. Honey

1 tbsp butter temp. environment

2 o 3 tbsp. white flour

In a bowl place 3 cups of rye flour with warm water and 10 g of yeast, mix and allow to stand covered with plastic for 24 hours.

To clear the air, stir the mixture and cover until the next day. Repeat until the third day.

On the fourth day add 1 cup hot water, 1 tablespoon of honey, 1 tablespoon of salt, 1 tablespoon of butter, 10 g of yeast and the remaining flour in half-cup measures until you have a firm, elastic dough.

Let it rise for 1 hour in an oiled bowl.

Form 2 or 3 rolls as ovals and place on rye floured trays. With beaten egg paint the surface and make cross-cuts on each about every 2 inches.

When it doubles in size put it in a hot oven for about 40 minutes or until it reaches a golden brown color

Pumpkin Bread

This bread is perfect for cooking in a clay oven

2 cups. boiled mashed pumpkin

1 cup boiling water (from boiling the pumpkin)

1 organic whole wheat flour (preferred)

½ tbsp. salt

½ tbsp. yeast

100 grs. butter

save the pumpkin seeds

To the still warm mash add the butter, water, a little flour to thicken the mixture and yeast. Stir to incorporate the ingredients and set aside.

Add to the mix the salt and flour kneed and let rise.

Divide into rolls and garnish with the washed and salted seeds. Place them on to a tray and place in the oven until muffins rise.

Beer Bread

Originally named "fermenter master" it is ideal to cook in a clay oven and enjoy with a home made beer

4 cups. fine rye flour	4 or 5 cups flour
1 lt. Premium Beer	10 grs. dry yeast
4 tbsp. corn oil	1 tbsp. coarse salt
2 tbsp honey	

In a saucepan warm the beer and add rye flour and yeast until it becomes a thick mixture.

Once it gains a spongy consitency, add the honey, salt and the remaining flour gradually. Stir with a wooden spoon until the mixture falls off of the walls of the pan. Then add the oil, and stir a while longer. Take it to the table and knead; let it rest with nylon and a cloth on top.

Once the dough has risen, cut 3 to 6 servings, make buns and let them rise, again covered. Give them the form of Zeppelins or place them into molds of your liking. You can decorate with poppy seeds too. When the buns have risen, place them in the oven at medium heat for about an hour.

Swedish Bread

Exquisite light rye crumbs, sweet and mentholated seeds

½ lt. of warm water	1 tbsp. yeast
2 cups. fine rye flour	2 tsp. coarse salt
2 tsp. Kümmel seeds	1 tbsp. Honey
2 tsp. anise seeds	3 cups. superfine white or wholemeal
Zest of 1/3 of an orange	¼ cup corn oil

With water, seeds, rye, yeast and a little superfine flour prepare a starter mix until thick and warm.

When it has become spongy incorporate the orange zest, salt, honey, more flour (gradually) and oil while kneading. Cover it with nylon and let rest.

When it has doubled in volume divide into 2 or 3 portions and make muffins with them, cover and leave to rest. When you see that they have relaxed, flatten and wrap them into a cylindrical shape. Leave to rise, make decorative cuts and take to the oven on medium heat (200 degrees) for one hour

Tynbrod

It was the seafaring cookie of the Vikings. Crisp and dry, they last for a long time

2 cups coarse rye flour

3 cups white wheat flour or wholemeal superfine

2 cups. Hot water

100 grs. butter

1 ½ tbsp. of fine salt

2 tbsp. kummel seed

1 tbsp. anise seed

1 tbsp. fennel seeds

50 grs. fresh yeast

Whisk water with seeds, yeast and butter. Add rye flour and let stand until foaming.

Adding wheat flour and salt until the mixture gradually separates from the walls of the bowl. Knead and let stand until risen.

With a rolling pin to stretch the dough to a thickness of 2 to 3 mm.

With a pastry cutter make circles or triangles and arrange on a platter. Wait until it rises then take to the oven on a high heat.

Rye Baguettes

Perfect for a picnic

Ingredients	Decoration
2 cups. finely ground rye	½ cup. de agua caliente
1 cup. coarse ground rye	1 tsp cornstarch or tapioca
2 cups. of warm water	1 teaspoon salt
1 tsp yeast	½ cup. coarse rye
2 tsp honey	
1 ½ tsp salt	
2 o 3 cups superfine whole wheat flour	
50 grs. butter	

Prepare a starting mixture with the rye flour, yeast and water. Let stand, covered, overnight in a warm place.

In the morning melt the honey with butter and salt in two tablespoons of water. When heated through, add the starter mix and stir. Next, clean the bowl with flour (later you add it to the dough).

Keep stirring and adding flour slowly until the dough becomes elastic to work it on the table.

Flour the table and knead until it does not stick to the surface: wrap with plastic and let stand until its volume has doubled.

Divide into portions of 200-300 grams and shape buns. Leave for a few minutes while you start to prepare the potato flour.

In a small bowl, place ½ cup of hot water, 1 teaspoon of salt and starch and take to the hob. Stir constantly on the stove until you feel that it is very thick. The potato flour can be used cold, hot and can also be preserved in the refrigerator for future loaves.

Return to the dough and shape sticks about 3 cm. in diameter.

Place on a floured tray and cover with plastic. Let stand in a warm place to rise.

When the baguettes soften a little paint them with the cornflour. Make diagonal cuts and decorate with coarse rye . Place in the oven on high heat until they turn golden brown and then after cooling enjoy with friends

SWEET BREADS

Twisted Filling

A simple shape and a surprise inside

Dough	Filling
200 cc. milk	300 grs. de Ricotta
1 tbsp. yeast	3 tbsp brown sugar
2 tbsp. sugar	1 tbsp. cinnamon
2 tbsp butter	4 tbsp. raisins
2 eggs	3 medium apples, diced
1 tsp salt	Zest 1 lemon
½ kg. flour 000	**Decoration**
	2 tbsp. Grand Marnier liqueur or other
	2 tbsp honey

In the warm milk dilute the yeast along with a cup of flour. Beat and allow to foam.

Separately mix the white butter, sugar and eggs then incorporates the above mixture gradually, with salt and flour. Stir with a wooden spoon until the mixture is ready to be kneaded.

Knead vigorously, split in two and let the dough rest covered with plastic and a cloth until doubled in volume.

While it rises prepare the filling. I advise you to warm the ricotta slightly to help with the last proofing. Then oil a tray.

Place dough on a floured board and flatten with your hands open first and then with a rolling pin until about 3 or 4 mm thick. In the center of mass (width) place the filling and wrap it alternating sides (covering the right side first and then take the left side and place it on the right). Wait until it rises and bring to the oven on medium heat until golden brown (about an hour).

After warming up, paint the surface with the combination of liquor and honey.

Wholewheat Croissants

This time we make croissants with classical mass of whole wheat flour, with the detail of a filling of butter to achieve a very original flavour and texture

1 well-kneaded common wholewheat bread dough (see recipe for basic dough)

Honey

300 grs. butter at room temperature

1 ½ cup. superfine wholewheat flour

With freshly kneaded dough form a bun. Let it rest on plastic until it leavens and can be worked.

Form a paste mixing it at a leisurely pace with the butter helping with a spatula, until you have a spreadable paste.

Flour the counter and place the dough on it. Flatten with hands to degas. With a rolling pin stretch the dough to a thickness of approximately 3 mm and give it a rectangular shape. So that it doesn't stick to the spatula or the table sprinkle with plenty of superfine flour.

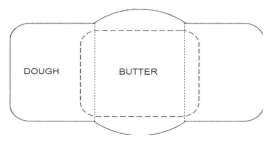

Spread a little more than half of the filling on the center strip of the dough rectangle.Close with the sides

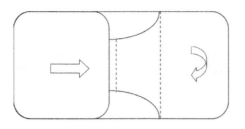

Repeat again rotating the dough a quarter turn and use the remainder of the filling.

Store in a plastic bag and take it to the refrigerator for 1 hour. On a floured board stretch and with a rolling pin roll to a thickness of 3 mm. Cut triangles

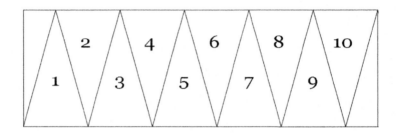

Roll up each triangle, give them the shape of crescents and place them on a greased pan.

Cover the dish with nylon and wait until it leavens again.

Bring the oven to a high heat and at about 15 minutes (or when they take some colour), take them out and paint with warm honey.

Ideal for filling them with ham and cheese and serve warm

OAT AND CHOCOLATE CRUNCHIES

Crunchies are more nutritious than other snacks, good to eat at any time!

1 ½ cup rolled oats	½ tsp. of fine salt
1 cup medium wholewheat flour	1 tbsp. baking powder
1 cup of chocolate chopped coarsely	½ cup milk
	1 ½ brown sugar
1 cup peeled and toasted sunflower seeds	150 grs. butter

Mix the flour, oats, baking powder and salt in a bowl. Add the sunflower seeds and chocolate.

In another bowl mix the soft butter with sugar and milk until creamy and add it to the mixture.

If you noticed that the mixture was too dry add milk until the dough is soft.

Stretch it into a tray to form a uniform layer of approximately 1 cm. thick

Place the dish in the oven on a medium heat until you see that it is barely cooked (about 20 minutes).

With a hot table knife cut rectangles and present them in a basket or on a wooden board.

Granola Nougat

Super energetic and healthy bars. You can replace the coconut with grated orange zest and carrots.

500 grs. of rolled oats	200 grams of raisins
100 grs. shredded coconut	200 chopped dried fruit (preferably pear, plum and fig)
100 grs. roasted peanuts	
100 grs. walnuts or almonds	400 grs. honey.

Take a heavy saucepan and place the first ingredients to toast until they turn golden. Reduce heat to low and stir while adding the second lot of ingredients until you get a smooth paste.

While the dough is still warm, press the dough into molds (you can use aluminum ice cube trays). Take them to the refrigerator until cool. Unmold and cut into smaller pieces. Present them wrapped in cellophane

APPLE CUPCAKES

250 cc water

50 grs. raisins (optional)

300 grs. de Honey

½ cup corn oil

2 eggs

1 ½ tsp baking powder

1 tsp salt

400 grs. flour 000

600 grs grams of green apples (diced)

14 custard aluminium cups disposable size 10

14 pirotines de paper N° 10

Mix the wet ingredients in a bowl, and in another bowl mix the dry ingredients. In a larger bowl place the diced and chopped apple.

Put in preheated oven at low heat. In a pan place the aluminum ramekins with paper mould in each.

Combine the apples with the wet mixture and add the dry mixture. Stir just a little, until the mixture is moist. Dump into the paper moulds with a spoon until the leading edge and baked.

The first 15 minutes should be at a low heat and leave for another 20 minutes over a high heat. To verify that the cooking is complete make sure the bottom is browned.

BAKED CAKES

2 cups water

1 kg. flour

10 grs. yeast

2 tsp. salt

2 tsp. sugar

200 grs soft butter

500 grs sweet quince or sweet potato

Syrup or honey

200 grs fresh cheese

With some of the flour, yeast and warm water prepare a starter mix. Knead the dough with the salt, sugar and the remaining flour.cover and leave to stand to rise.

Add to the butter 1 ½ cups of flour to get a spreadable paste.

Once the dough has risen, stretch on a floured surface to a thickness of 2 mm.In the centre smear with dough and fold the edges joining them in the middle. Repeat the procedure. Put it to one side, let it rise and stretch again.

Prepare the sweet quince in square slices of about 4 cm wide. Cut the dough into squares of about 7 cm long. Place the slices of sweet quince and a piece of cheese in the centre, pinch the tips to form the pastry.

Arrange them on a greased tray and cover with a nylon quickly to rise a little more.

Bake at very high heat. Once browned remove from the oven and brush with syrup or honey

STUFFED BREADS

Humita stuffed Bread

Ingredients	**Filling**
4 cups water	Boiled corn
10 cup superfine flour	Pure Pumpkin
1 tbsp. yeast and honey or sugar spoon	Fresh cheese
1 tbsp. coarse salt	Salt and ground pepper to taste
½ cup oil	

Prepare a startup mix as indicated in basic techniques.

Knead the surplus flour with salt and honey. Leave to rise covered with nylon. Leave to one side

fresh cheese. Season with salt and red pepper remembering that the flavour lessens by being in the dough.

With a rolling pin stretch and cut rectangles to cover the filling.

Place them on a floured tray covered with nylon and wait until they rise. Bake on high heat.

Once the baked breads are out of the oven arrange them in a basket and cover with fabric to keep them hot for a couple of hours.

BREAD STUFFED WITH CHORIZO

6 Chorizos or grill sausages (with skin)

1 kg. flour

1 tbsp. yeast

½ tbsp. salt

1 tbsp. sugar

600 cc warm water

On the table to form a ring of flour, pour in the liquid mixture and add salt. Stir gradually incorporating the flour from the edges. Knead to form a bun with no cracks and let the dough rest to rise.

Take a rolling pin and stretch the dough to a thickness of 0.5 cm and divide it into 6 equal portions. With each serving wrap the Chorizos and tie the edges of the dough with a thread on the tips. Oil a roasting pan, arrange them and bring to high heat or until the dough is soft.

Ideal to serve as a starter to a meat dish

HAM TORZADAS

1 kg. salt dough

100 grs. grated cheese

200 grs. de cooked ham
(cut into slices)

Let the salt dough rise.

Flour the table, flatten dough with hands first and then spread it with a rolling pin until you have a thickness of 2 or 3 mm. Oil a platter and put to one side.

Take the cheese and sprinkle on the table. Wet your hand, moisten only one side of the dough and place that surface carefully on the table with grated cheese. On top place the ham.

Make sticks 3 or 4 inches with a roller for cutting pizza or ravioli. Take care not to drag the dough beneath.

To make the plait take each rectangle, keeping one end rested and fold the other diagonally.

You can let them rise or cook immediately. The oven must be on a high heat until they have browned.

STUFFED CROISSANTS

Ingredients

2 tsp dry yeast

¾ litre cream

1 egg

1 tbsp salt

1 tbsp sugar

½ cup butter

5 cups flour 000

Mocha Cream Filling

4 tbsp. butter

5 tbsp. powdered sugar

2 tsp cocoa powder

2 tbsp instant coffee

Apple Stuffing

2 boiled pureed apples

½ cup raisins

Separate 5 tablespoons flour in a bowl and set aside.

Place remaining flour in another bowl with the salt and form a hole. While beating, add the warm cream, the yeast and egg (previously mixed in another container). Add part of the flour until you get a thick cream. Stir in butter with reserved flour joining them with a fork.

Dump the yeast mixture over the mixture and stir to incorporate the flour from the edges gradually until it becomes an elastic dough.

Put it on the table and knead with the flour that was left for 10 minutes.

FESTIVE

BREADS

Pretzel

500 grs. flour

1 tsp salt

1 tbsp sugar

1 tbsp dry yeast

250 cc of warm milk

50 grs. butter

Coarse salt

Mix flour, yeast, sugar and salt. Add warm milk to the mixture until the dough is homogeneous. Cover it, let it rest in a warm place for about 15 minutes and then add the butter at room temperature.

Kneed, and in case you need to, add a tablespoon of flour so the dough is smooth and not sticking to your hands. Leave covered to rise until doubled in size.

Degas and form in to the characteristic figure of pretzels:

Sprinkle the table with semi-fine or coarse ground salt. Form a thin stick of approximately 70 cm long and knead on top of the salt to make it impregnate into the dough. Make a Pretzel shape.

CORN BREAD

.Ideal for eating hot accompanied with a good red wine

200 grs. cornmeal	1 tsp sugar
300 grs. all-purpose flour	150 cc of water
1 large red bell pepper	25 gr. compressed yeast
2 tsp salt	50 cc of olive oil
1 tsp of ground pepper	50 cc corn oil

In water with oil dissolve the yeast by beating well. Chop the bell pepper into small pieces. In a bowl put all dry ingredients and mix. Combine all of them and knead the mix. Cover with a nylon until risen.

Divide into rolls of 3 cm in diameter. Sprinkle corn flour on a platter and arrange them. Cover them and let them rise. Bring the oven to high heat and wait until they are golden brown.

Enjoy them with friends.

OAT AND BEER TORTILLAS

Delight to eat on their own, with sweet or savoury dishes

250 grs. rolled oats

2 eggs

400 cc of beer

1 tbsp. yeast

1 tsp salt

1 tbsp. sugar

50 grs butter for frying

Join the yeast with warm beer and let it stand for a few minutes.

Add remaining ingredients and whisk vigorously. Let rest for about 2 hours. Heat a frying pan (about 15 cm) over low heat with a little butter and pour the mixture with a spoon to coat the bottom. When the dough takes a brown colour turn it over with a spatula so that it cooks on the other side.

After a couple of minutes frying place them on a wooden plate and cover with a cloth to serve warm.

BAGEL

ewish bread with an interesting technique

400 grams of flour	1 tsp salt
3 tsp dry yeast	1 egg
250 cc of milk	3 liters. boiling water
¼ cup Corn oil	Poppy seeds for garnish

Place 75 grams of flour in a large bowl and add the yeast. Add the warm milk and whisk well. Let the mixture sit for about 10 minutes. Add the oil, egg and salt integrating with a wooden spoon until the mixture is homogeneous.

Stir in remaining flour gradually and mix with hands until you get a fine dense dough. Knead until it's elastic and gives freely.

oil a bowl, and cover the dough with nylon. Let it rise for about 45 to 50 minutes.

Make small buns and make a hole in the centre with your thumb. Straighten the edges a bit if necessary.

Let stand and put to boil water with a pinch of baking soda. When doubled in volume place them on a strainer and submerge them en water a few minutes. Drain them on a plate, sprinkle with seeds and bake

Special Focaccia

In the focaccia white flour is used, but this is special. It turned out to be an oily and salty bread. Not recommended for the hypertensive person

Ingredients	**Decoration**
50 grs. Fresh yeast	2 tsp salt semi-fine
1 tsp honey	6 tablespoons olive oil
1 tsp salt	Sprigs of fresh rosemary
2 tsp dried rosemary	
1 tbsp sunflower oil	
1 ½ cups superfine flour	
½ cup mid flour	

In a cup of warm water dissolve yeast, honey and rosemary. Allow to froth and incorporate the oil, salt and flour gradually. Kneed and leave to one side to rise.

Divide in two and flatten to a pizza shape. Oil a platter, wet the surface of the dough and sprinkle with semi-fine salt. Leave to rise.

Make deep holes with your fingers and rub with olive oil. Then take to the oven to on a high heat.

RICE BREAD

Great for those who like macrobiotics: High proportion of rice to flour make these breads low in gluten

2 cups coarsely ground brown rice (preferably Yamanî)	½ tbsp. dry yeast
	1 tbsp. corn oil
1 cup. superfine flour	½ tbsp honey
3 cups water	½ tsp salt

Take the rice and grind it in a mortar or blender until it resembles coarse sand. Bring a pot of salted water to the boil and boil it. Stir with wooden spoon and immediately turn off the heat to achieve a half cooked state.

Once warm add a little flour, honey and, if necessary, another cup of water. The mixture should be creamy but thick, that is, that by taking a scoop and drop it on the dough it does not dissolve.

Sprinkle in the yeast and stir to incorporate. Leave it to rise a bit. In the case that the mass is liquefied by yeast, add ½ cup of flour. Spoon into oiled moulds.

Take to the oven until risen.

BREAD BAKING BIBLE

For Bread Bakers Apprentice

Maru Castilla

Made in United States
North Haven, CT
29 November 2023

44752301R00046